COMPUTER GAME AND FILM GRAPHICS

Paul Byrne

H www.heinemann.co.uk/library
Visit our website to find out more information about Heinemann Library books.

To order:
📞 Phone 44 (0) 1865 888066
📄 Send a fax to 44 (0) 1865 314091
💻 Visit the Heinemann Bookshop at www.heinemann.co.uk/library to browse our catalogue and order online.

Produced for Heinemann Library by
White-Thomson Publishing Ltd,
Bridgewater Business Centre,
210 High Street, Lewes,
East Sussex BN7 2NH.

First published in Great Britain by Heinemann Library,
Jordan Hill, Oxford OX2 8EJ, part of Harcourt Education.
Heinemann Library is a registered trademark of
Harcourt Education Ltd.

© Harcourt Education Ltd 2007

The moral right of the proprietor has been asserted.

Editorial: Clare Collinson, Melanie Waldron, Kate Buckingham
Consultant: Susie Hodge
Design: Tim Mayer
Picture Research: Amy Sparks
Production: Chroma Graphics

Originated by Modern Age Ltd
Printed and bound in China by South China Printing Company.

10 digit ISBN: 0 431 01474 4
13 digit ISBN: 978-0-431-01474-6

11 10 09 08 07
10 9 8 7 6 5 4 3 2

British Library Cataloguing in Publication Data
Byrne, P.
  Computer games and film graphics. – (Art off the wall)
  794.8'166
A full catalogue record for this book is available from the
British Library.

Acknowledgements
The publisher would like to thank the following for their kind permission to use their photographs:
akg-images pp. **6**, **9** (Warner Bros. Pictures/Album), **11** (Walt Disney Productions/Album), **14** (Universal Studios/Album), **20–21** (Lucas Film/JAK Productions/Album), **25** (Lucas Film/Album), **26** (DreamWorks Pictures/Album), **27** (Walt Disney Pictures/Album), **28–29** (DreamWorks Pictures/Album), **30** (New Line Productions/Album), **31** (Universal Pictures/Album), **32** (United Artists/Keith Hamshere/Album), **33** (Fox Animation Studios/Blue Sky Studios/Album), **39** (New Line Cinema/The Saul Zaentz); Alamy pp. **12** (Sinibomb Images), **18** (James Quine), **46–47** (Iain Masterton), **48** (Michael Booth); Corbis pp. **10** (Close Murray/Corbis Sygma), **35** (DreamWorks SKG/ZUMA), **42** (Louie Psihoyos), **50** (Bill Varie), Electronic Arts Inc. pp. **5**, **7**, **13**, **15**, **16**, **17**, **21**, **24**, **34**; Getty Images pp. **19** (AFP), **36–37** (AFP), **38** (AFP), **40–41** (AFP), **44**, **45** (AFP), **51**; Science Photo Library pp. **22** (Simon Fraser/Mari), **23** (Alfred Pasieka); TopFoto pp. **4** (Topham Picturepoint), **9**, **43** (Topham Picturepoint), **49** (ImageWorks).

Cover photograph reproduced with permission of Science Photo Library.

Every effort has been made to contact copyright
holders of any material reproduced in this book.
Any omissions will be rectified in subsequent
printings if notice is given to the publishers.

Contents

Words appearing in the text in bold, **like this**, are explained in the Glossary.

Computer game and film graphics

When you are playing your favourite computer game or watching the latest **special effects** in a blockbuster film, you are looking at artwork created with **computer graphics**.

In modern films, many of the images you see, including the realistic-looking landscapes, buildings, vehicles, and even the characters, are created as computer graphics. Almost everything you see in modern computer games is produced from artwork made using computers. This kind of artwork is called computer-generated imagery, or **CGI** for short.

Computer-generated imagery

CGI is artwork that is made, or generated, using computers. It is important to know that this artwork is not created by computers – it is created by artists.

The term CGI often refers only to the highly detailed artwork used to create special effects in many modern films such as *The Lord of the Rings* or *Star Wars* and cartoons such as *Shrek* and *The Incredibles*. The term CGI can also also refer to the artwork used in computer and video games. In this book, we will talk about both these forms of CGI.

The character Gollum from *The Lord of the Rings* is one of the finest examples of computer-generated art ever created.

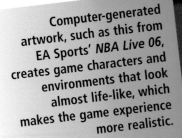

Computer-generated artwork, such as this from EA Sports' *NBA Live 06*, creates game characters and environments that look almost life-like, which makes the game experience more realistic.

A growing industry

Some of the CGI created by today's artists is among the most awe-inspiring modern art you'll find. It is the final product of a process that often involves whole teams of artists – painters, illustrators, sculptors, and animators – working on projects for months and even years. A career as an artist in the CGI industry is one of the most exciting and rewarding jobs you can find. And the great news is that CGI is a growing industry that offers many opportunities for the artists of the future.

Skills and techniques

In this book, you will learn about the basics of CGI. There will be examples of the skills and techniques artists use to create this amazing art. You will also learn about the various types of artwork that are created as part of the CGI process, such as simple **concept art**, paintings, sculptures, and **storyboards**.

Try it yourself

Throughout this book, you will find activities that you can try yourself. These are simple exercises to do with particular stages in the CGI process. The aim is for you to build up your skills so you can get started in the fascinating world of art for computer games and films.

The three-dimensional world

A herd of dinosaurs charges right at you as you sit watching a film. They look so realistic that you are sure the beasts are going to break through the screen. In the fantasy world of your favourite computer game, you feel as if you are inside the game. These experiences are possible through the magic of computer-generated three-dimensional (**3D**) artwork.

The third dimension

What is the difference between space that is 3D and space that is two-dimensional (**2D**)? Two dimensions are what you have on a flat surface, such as a tabletop, a sheet of paper, or a video screen. These two dimensions are height and width. The space we live in, however, is three-dimensional – it has height and width, and it also has depth.

The evolution of art

The earliest known examples of art, such as cave drawings or ancient Egyptian paintings, look flat and unnatural because they give no sense of depth. By the 15th century, artists had learned the rules of **perspective** to create the **illusion** of depth and distance in their flat, two-dimensional paintings.

Artists also learned how to use light, shadows, shading, and subtle changes in colour to create a sense of depth and make objects in their paintings seem solid and real.

By the 1400s, artists had learned to create the illusion of three dimensions in their paintings by following the rules of perspective. In this 15th-century painting by the Dutch artist Jan Van Eyck, the tower appears far in the distance.

Traditional art skills and CGI

Of course, everything you see in a painting or drawing is the same distance away from you. Any depth you think you see in a drawing or painting is only an illusion. The same is true when you think you see three dimensions on a flat, two-dimensional television or computer screen, or on a cinema screen.

Artists who create artwork for computer games and films need to learn how to use perspective, light, shadows, shading, and colours to create the illusion of three dimensions. They must master many of the same skills as traditional artists.

The artist who created this shot from EA's *Need For Speed: Most Wanted* had a thorough knowledge of perspective. The car appears to be right in front of us and the buildings seem far off in the distance.

Try it yourself

Here is a simple way of creating the illusion of a 3D object on a 2D surface. All you will need is a pencil, a ruler, and some paper.

1 First, using your ruler, draw a square.

2 Now draw a small dot in the centre of your square and draw a straight line between this dot and the bottom left corner of your square.

3 Next, from the three remaining corners, draw three more lines that are exactly the same length and angle as the last line you drew.

4 As a final step, draw another square that connects the ends of your four lines. Now you have created the illusion of a 3D cube.

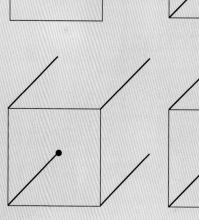

Digital artwork

Armed with the skills of a traditional artist, a **digital** artist uses the added power of computers. Computer software allows artists to create images that are impossible to achieve with traditional art techniques.

Some computer graphics for games and films are made up of 2D artwork copied from real drawings or 2D illustrations drawn directly on to the computer. Just like a traditional artist, the digital artist's goal is usually to create the illusion of three dimensions through the use of perspective and subtle changes in light, shadows, and colour. The tools provided by computer software help digital artists add these illusions to their 2D artwork.

Digital light

As in other forms of art such as painting and drawing, digital artists need to be very creative in the way they use light and shadows to make their artwork appear realistic. The light we see in games and film graphics is artificial light, so the trick is to make this virtual light appear natural as characters and objects move through the three-dimensional world of computer-generated imagery.

3D graphics software

The most innovative art made for computer games and films is created with 3D graphics software. This software allows digital artists to go beyond the 2D world of traditional art and 2D computer software such as *Photoshop*, and into a **virtual** 3D world.

Digital models

Using 3D software, artists create **digital models**. These digital models may be built for characters, vehicles, buildings, and entire environments that appear in a computer game or film. Unlike a 2D illustration, which is a flat image, a 3D computer model is created with the shapes and dimensions of real objects. Think of the difference between a drawing and a sculpture: the drawing is flat, but the sculpture has a real shape to it and can be viewed from different sides. A digital 3D model is a lot like a sculpture or a statue, even though it exists only in the virtual world of the computer. You can read more about how 3D models are created on pages 22–23.

Making digital models seem real

Because digital 3D models are built with the shapes of real objects, they can be made to look much more realistic than 2D illustrations.

But creating digital 3D models is only one stage in the process of making the images seem realistic. Once they are created, models then need to be animated, or moved according to their roles in a computer game or film. Computer **animation** is an art form that we'll discuss further as we move into the process of creating CGI.

The way light and shadows are used in computer-generated images, such as this image from the animated film *The Polar Express*, is very important in the creation of a realistic-looking 3D environment.

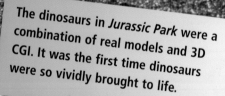
The dinosaurs in *Jurassic Park* were a combination of real models and 3D CGI. It was the first time dinosaurs were so vividly brought to life.

Movie magic

Computer-generated special effects in films and television have been around for over 40 years. The film *Futureworld*, made in 1976, was the first major film to use 3D CGI. But it was not until the late 1980s that computer-generated special effects first appeared as **photorealistic 3D art alongside real actors in live-action films.** When we say something is photorealistic, it simply means that it is life-like and looks as real as something would appear in a photograph.

The 1989 film *The Abyss* featured a photorealistic 3D "water creature", created entirely using 3D computer-generated imagery. A few years later, CGI was used in the film *Jurassic Park* to create dinosaurs that interacted with real actors in a way that made them seem very believable and real. Today's computer graphics artistry has progressed even further. Many recent films, such as *The Lord of the Rings*, *Star Wars III: Revenge of the Sith*, and *King Kong*, could not have been made without 3D CGI.

Computer-generated environments

In today's films the human characters may be the only things that are real within an environment that has been created entirely using CGI. Every scene in *Star Wars III: Revenge of the Sith* includes at least some CGI. The actors in today's films are often filmed in front of a giant screen (coloured blue or green), and the surrounding environment in which the actors will eventually be seen in the film is created with computers.

Fully animated films

Not all CGI is used to create photorealistic special effects. Some of the most entertaining forms of computer-generated art have been fully animated films such as *Shrek*, *Monsters Inc.*, and *The Incredibles*.

CGI is used in these films to create complete fantasy worlds with highly detailed characters that viewers can believe in, even though we know they are not real. Every part of these animated films, from characters and buildings to grass and sky, is created using computer graphics.

Toy Story featured a full cast of highly detailed 3D models who look and move remarkably like real toys.

Toy Story

The 1995 film *Toy Story*, was the first feature-length film that was animated entirely using computers. This blockbuster film was the first major release from Pixar Animation Studios, who went on to create other CGI films, including *Monsters Inc.*, *Finding Nemo*, and *Cars*. You can read more about Pixar on pages 42–43.

Art in computer games

Many of the tools and techniques used to make computer-generated artwork for characters and environments in live-action and animated films are also used to create the 3D characters and fantasy worlds you see in today's video and computer games.

The first-ever computer game was *Spacewar*, which appeared in 1961. One of the first games to reach a large audience was *Pong*, which was released in 1972. The game consisted of two rectangles on either side of the screen that were used like tennis rackets to hit a square "ball" back and forth.

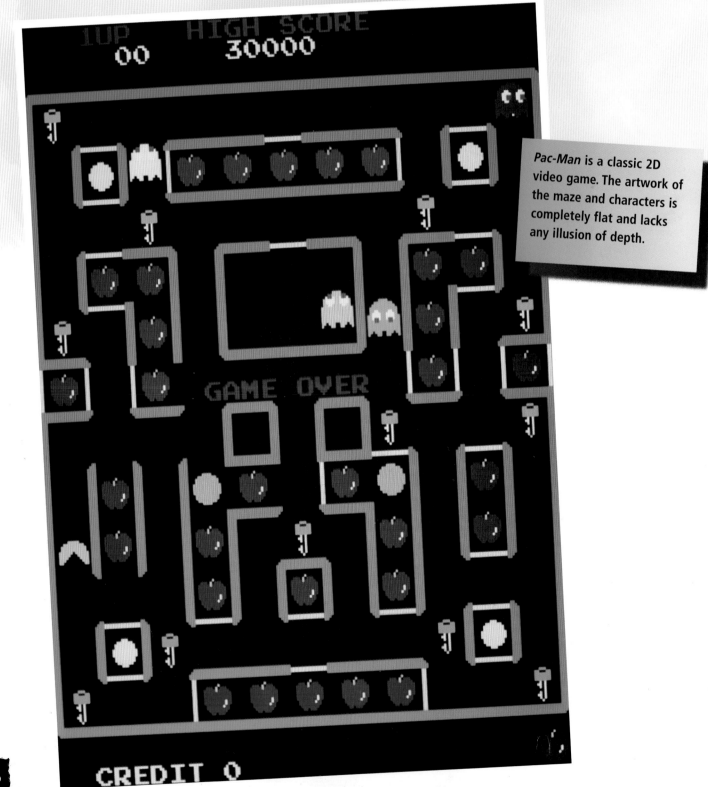

Pac-Man is a classic 2D video game. The artwork of the maze and characters is completely flat and lacks any illusion of depth.

2D computer games

Later in the 1970s, with the release of the Atari 2600 home game console, video games became more popular. Millions of children could now play games such as *Space Invaders*, *Donkey Kong*, and *Pac-Man* in their own living rooms.

Artwork in these early computer games was limited to poorly defined images. These early games were 2D, so a player could move only up, down, and across the screen.

3D computer games

Computer game graphics have developed rapidly since the early days. As graphics became sharper and more highly defined, games featuring 3D artwork began to appear. In today's auto racing games, you speed through highly defined 3D environments. Combat games often show the battlefield as seen from the infantryman's point of view. Sports games have players that look almost like real athletes. It is the 3D artwork in these games that makes the experience so realistic. Some of the newest games feature graphics that are so detailed you can almost count the blades of grass on a virtual golf course or football field!

Moving in three dimensions

A player in a 3D computer game can move in what seems to be three dimensions. As in the first computer games, a player is still only moving up, down, and across a two-dimensional screen, but the 3D artwork that surrounds and interacts with a player on-screen makes it seem as if the player is in a 3D environment. The player appears to move "forward" or "into the game", but often the player stays in almost the same position on-screen. It is the whole 3D environment that moves around the player. This gives the illusion that the player is moving through a 3D environment.

From Concept to Computer

The computer-generated images we see in computer games and films often take a long time to develop. This chapter describes the early stages of the process and introduces the various types of artwork that are involved in the development of computer graphics.

Story

All artwork that is created for computer games and films begins with a story, or perhaps even a simple idea. A story gives artists ideas about the kinds of art that are needed for a given project. A story comes in the form of a script for a film or game. The script describes the basic storyline or plot, introduces the characters, and describes the action that takes place.

Computer game and film graphics artists use their talents to take the words of the scriptwriter, and add their own interpretations to the characters and environments to create artwork that will best tell the writer's story.

These detailed illustrations and this model were created at the early stages of the CGI process for the 2001 film, *The Mummy Returns*.

Concept art

The first artwork created in the CGI process is concept art. Concept art comes in many forms. It can be anything from simple, pencil-drawn sketches on paper to highly detailed sculptures of characters or coloured paintings of an entire fantasy environment for a game or film scene.

This traditional artwork provides basic visualizations of what will later be created on computers. It also allows the team of artists working together on a project to consider a number of different versions and possibilities and to choose the characters and images that work best before any work is done on computers.

This concept artwork of goblin spiders from EA's *The Lord of the Rings: Battle for Middle Earth II* shows how drawings can help visualize ideas for characters.

Try it yourself

For this exercise, you just need to think of a basic storyline from one of your favourite books. Once you have thought of your story, choose a single part of the plot – this will be your "scene" to work on as a concept artist. Try to sketch a few images from the scene, such as characters or structures, a landscape or an overall environment. Don't worry about the details of your sketches – it is more important at this stage that you just visualize some basic ideas. As a concept artist, you interpret the story as you see it in your own mind.

Character sketches

The characters you see in computer game and film graphics usually start as simple sketches on paper. Artists use pencils, pens, or markers to draw character outlines. These just give the basic idea of how a character will look. A team of artists will often create a number of possibilities showing how a character might appear, and a selection process will decide which version they prefer. Artists often create more detailed illustrations or paintings of main characters as the ideas for these characters become more defined. You can read more about the development of characters on pages 20–21.

Environmental concept art

The idea for a fantasy environment in a game or film starts with the story, but it is artists who provide the first vision of what the environment will look like. Simple pencil sketches can be a good start, but environmental concept art may consist of richly detailed, coloured paintings or illustrations. The vibrant colours in these paintings and illustrations act as a guide for later stages in the process.

Practical models

As well as drawing sketches, artists often create sculptures of characters and models of environments with clay or other materials. These sculptures and models are often very detailed to provide a precise example of what is to be created on computers. Sculptures are sometimes created as **maquettes**. These are finely detailed sculptures depicting a character in a particular pose for a single moment in a film. These maquettes can be copied when virtual character models are created on computers at a later stage (see page 23).

Inspiration

Artists working on computer games and films find inspiration from many different sources. They may be inspired by drawings, paintings, and photographs of landscapes, which give them ideas for fantasy environments for computer games or film scenes. Drawings and paintings of buildings may provide them with ideas about how ancient ruins or a modern cityscape might look in a fantasy world.

This character sketch is an archer from EA's *The Lord of the Rings: Battle for Middle Earth II*. Although it is just a drawing, it shows us a great deal about this character.

A wide view of the elf city Rivendell from *The Lord of the Rings* shows how this environment might look in the computer game.

Try it yourself

Take a look at some of the sketches you drew for the previous exercise on page 15. Choose just one or two sketches to develop a bit further. If you are working with a character sketch, add details such as clothing and defined facial expressions. If you are working on an environmental sketch, decide what kind of colours and lighting belong in the environment based on the story being told. These are the kinds of things artists must work out in the early stages of the CGI process.

Storyboards

The creation of storyboards is a very important stage in producing computer-generated art. Storyboards usually consist of a series of rough sketches showing a planned scene. Each sketch shows the main action within a single moment of a scene. When the sketches are put together one after the other, they provide a basic visual idea of how a scene will look from one moment to the next.

Storyboards are a bit like **comic strips**, but there are no words to explain what the characters are thinking or what else is happening – only images. Storyboards take the concept art stage a step further by showing how characters and other elements will come together as the story is being acted out.

It is important that storyboard artists show not only any action that is taking place, but also the changing emotions of characters as the action happens. These emotional changes in the characters can be represented by different facial expressions and body postures.

Storyboards illustrate the action within each moment of a story. Notice how some of the pictures are crossed out – these are images that probably didn't make it to the final film or game.

Getting it right

The storyboard stage allows a team of artists to see and agree upon how a scene will work before they go into actual production on computers. During this part of the process artists can come up with ideas to improve upon the story, and it is not too late to make changes.

A team of artists reviews storyboard pictures to decide which ones can be improved, and which ones may not be needed for a scene.

Try it yourself

Try creating a storyboard for the following scene. An explorer on a distant planet is on the run from enemy aliens and must reach his spaceship before they catch him. Your task is to create a storyboard showing how the scene will appear on-screen.

1 Start with a close-up sketch of the explorer, showing his emotional expressions and body movement as he is on the run.

2 In the next sketch, zoom out from your close-up to show the explorer within the surrounding environment.

3 With the next sketch, you might show a group of aliens in pursuit.

4 Then, go back to the explorer and show him within sight of his spaceship.

5 Now show another close-up of the explorer, relieved to be inside the spaceship and getting ready to take off.

6 The last sketch can show the spaceship taking off, leaving the aliens in a cloud of dust.

As an alternative to this scene, you may want to work with the story and characters from your previous activities. The important thing is that you show how a scene will look as it unfolds.

In the 1980s *Star Wars* films, Yoda was a real puppet. The Jedi master was recreated as a digital character for Episodes I, II, and III. This scene shows the digital version of Yoda from *Star Wars Episode II: Attack of the Clones*.

Making characters believable

Characters are often the most important feature of a story or game experience. The story is told through the words, emotions, and actions of characters. Whether a character is an enemy combatant in a computer game, a cartoon hero in an animated feature film, or a digital addition to a live-action film, the most important thing is that the character seems believable. The viewer or gamer must believe in the characters on-screen in order for the experience to seem like the real thing.

Character development

Some characters may go through a number of changes while they are being developed by a team of concept artists. Sometimes, detailed information about a character's appearance is included in a story or script, but artists often have the freedom to decide how a character should look based a rough description. For example, the story may simply call for "an insect-like alien". It is then up to the team of concept artists to build upon that idea and create a defined character.

Avatars

An avatar is a digital image or icon selected or created by Internet users to represent themselves in instant messaging and emails. Avatars can be customized, so users can choose the features they want. When customizing your avatar you have a choice of facial expressions showing various emotions (happiness, sadness, anger, etc.). You must also choose hair and skin colour, as well as the type of clothes your avatar wears. This is a good exercise in character development. As you customize an avatar's appearance, mood, and personality, you make decisions that any character developer would make.

As they are creating characters, artists need to decide not only about a character's appearance. They must also dig deeper and think about how a character behaves and how the character is involved in the story. This helps artists create a real personality for each character, so the characters appear more realistic.

Believe it or not, this is not a photograph of Tiger Woods. It is a digital double of Tiger created for EA Sports' *PGA 2006* game.

Character doubles

Some characters created using CGI are meant to look like real people. Some sports games feature digital models of actual athletes who may look like the real person. Character models are also created as "digital stunt doubles" to replace real actors for computer-generated scenes in live-action films.

3D computer modelling

Once the environmental setting and the appearance and personality of the characters have been agreed upon, it is time to move on to the computer modelling stage. It is at this stage that environmental concept art, character sketches, and physical models are transformed into virtual 3D models within the computer.

Wire frame structures

Three-dimensional computer models are usually created as virtual **wire frame** structures. A wire frame structure represents the outer shape of a character or other object. This wire frame looks a bit like a mesh or web covering the entire surface of the character or object. The mesh is made up of small shapes such as triangles. These shapes are arranged by digital modellers to form the unique shapes and dimensions of each 3D model.

Arranging 3D shapes

To create a wire frame mesh, a 3D modeller begins with a basic three-dimensional shape, such as a sphere, which the 3D software provides as a starting point. The 3D model gradually takes shape as the modeller adjusts and stretches the various points and lines in the wire frame mesh. For example, a modeller who needs to create a volcano may start with a cone-shaped wire frame structure. The modeller can gradually rearrange the points and lines in the smooth surface of the cone to resemble the jagged, lava-scarred surface of a volcano.

Virtual 3D objects are created using 3D computer software. A wire frame mesh is altered to create the shape of a character or environmental model.

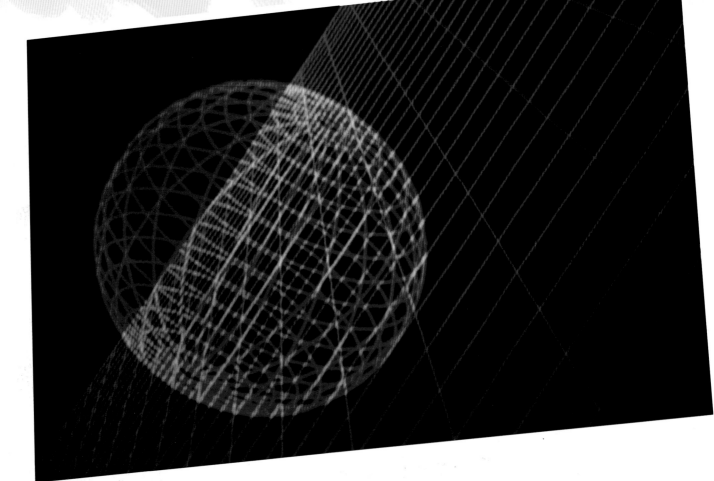

Wire frame models can be formed into any shape needed. Notice how the triangular sections of the wire frame become smaller to create details in the ears and around the eyes.

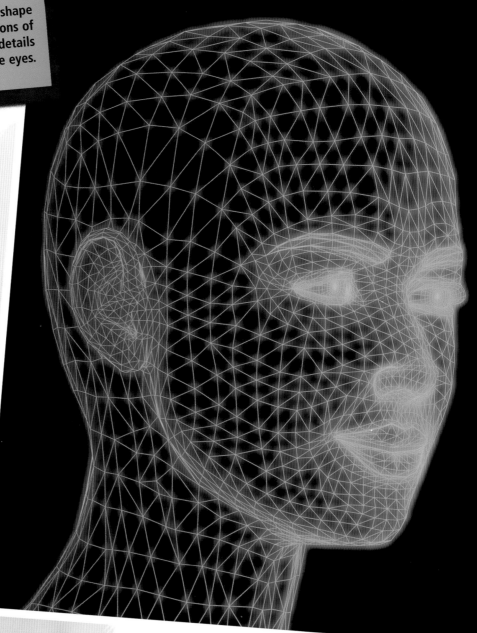

Virtual character models

Wire frame models for some computer-generated environments and objects consist just of an outer wire frame mesh. However, wire frame models of characters usually consist of an outer wire frame mesh attached to an inner virtual stick model.

A virtual stick model acts a bit like a wire skeleton. Every part of the stick model is defined with coordinates, a bit like map coordinates, that are keyed into the computer. For example, a stick model of a human leg will have coordinates for the hip, knee, and ankle. These coordinates act as control points that will be used when the character is made to move (see pages 28–29).

Once the inner stick model of a digital character has been created, the outer shape can be formed using a wire frame mesh. Just as in other wire frame structures, the points of the mesh can be pieced together and rearranged to form the overall shape of the character.

An easier way

Modellers can sometimes take shortcuts, if they have the right tools. Detailed character sculptures or other real objects can be scanned using lasers that measure the exact dimensions of the sculptured model. This 3D scan can then be loaded into the computer and turned into a virtual 3D model so that modellers do not have to start from scratch.

Building a computer-generated environment

Each scene in a film may have its own unique environmental setting. In a computer game, the various levels in the game may also have their own environmental setting. In some games, the player can choose different environments. For example, a player may be able to choose between various different types of golf course or different racetracks. Each of these computer-generated environments needs to be built by digital artists.

Game environments like this one are built from 3D models. Each of these shapes and structures began as a wire frame model and were pieced together into the fantasy world we see here.

2D backdrops

Three-dimensional models are important in creating realistic-looking 3D computer-generated environments. However, some of the art used to create backgrounds for computer games and films may be in the form of 2D digital illustrations.

Environmental elements such as sky and clouds or distant landscapes are often created as 2D art and used as backdrops in combination with 3D artwork.

Virtual environment models

Computer-generated environments are often created entirely from virtual 3D models. Virtual wire frame structures may be created for all parts of the environment and all the objects within it, such as buildings, trees, and mountains. The interiors of buildings and any objects within them may also be created as virtual 3D structures.

In computer games this 3D artwork allows the player to move within a realistic environment and interact with 3D objects, which can be seen from different points of view. Artists must make sure that objects within the game environment look right from every possible view available to the player.

Photorealistic environments in films

While the environments within games and fully animated films are often made entirely of 3D models and 2D illustrations, photorealistic environments in live-action films may actually be created from a combination of photographs of the real world mixed in with digital models and illustrations.

Case study: Mustafar

In *Star Wars III: Revenge of the Sith* Mustafar is the lava planet where Anakin Skywalker and Obi-Wan Kenobi confront each other. The digital artists who created Mustafar found images from the real world that helped them build this photorealistic fantasy environment. Some of the exploding lava that we see in these scenes is actual video footage of lava shooting out of Mt. Etna, a volcano in Sicily that happened to be erupting while the film was being made. Another image used to create Mustafar was a photograph of a gravel car park just outside the studio in San Francisco, California, where the CGI for the film was being made. The rough texture of the gravel served perfectly as the surface of this fictional volcanic world.

The digital environment of Mustafar was a combination of 2D illustrations, physical models, virtual 3D models, photographs, and live film, all pieced together to form a visually stunning world.

STAR WARS

Bringing graphics to life

In the last chapter we discussed how artists develop the early stages of computer graphics for games and films. Now we'll find out how concept art and computer models are turned into the moving images we see on-screen.

Creating movement

How can computer-generated characters in live-action films be made to move so realistically alongside real actors? And how can virtual characters in fully animated films move so naturally, with gestures that are so convincing and life-like that you believe they are real? Bringing 3D computer-generated images to life requires animation carried out by computer animators.

Traditional hand-drawn animation

The art of animation is in creating the illusion of movement using a series of still images. Traditional hand-drawn animation is made by filming a series of single illustrations, which are changed slightly from one drawing to the next. When these drawings are viewed very quickly one after the other, they give the illusion of movement. A special camera is used to film each image, called a frame. In most animated films, the frames are shown at 24 frames per second or faster to help make the movement appear smooth and realistic.

Stop motion

The illusion of movement can also be created using **stop motion** animation, which involves traditional models, such as clay figures, instead of drawings on paper. The models are put in position, photographed, and then moved slightly before being photographed again. When the frames are shown in quick succession, the models appear to move.

Wallace and Gromit: The Curse of the Were-Rabbit was made with real 3D models animated with stop motion techniques.

Computer animation

Computer animation is similar to stop motion animation, but it uses virtual 3D computer models instead of real models. Similar to the way that clay models are moved slightly between one frame and the next, the position of computer-generated models is moved slightly between frames by computer animators.

Why not try creating a simple traditional animation? All you need is a pencil and a notebook. On the back page of your notebook, draw a simple stick figure (think of this as a single frame). Then, working from the back page towards the front, draw the same figure in a way that shows movement from one page to the next. For example, place your stick character's limbs in slightly different positions from one drawing to the next. You can then flip through the pages to view a simple animation.

If you have access to a digital camera, you can make your own simple stop motion animation using figures such as Lego characters. Move the characters slightly from one picture to the next, and then play back the pictures as a slideshow.

Unlike traditional animation, which is created with 2D illustrations, computer-generated animation like that in *Monsters Inc.* is created using 3D CGI.

Animating characters

A speciality within the field of computer animation is character animation, which is the art of bringing a virtual character to life. Character animators must make their characters move naturally. They also need to show facial expressions and different emotions in a way that appears believable and realistic.

Different facial expressions and body postures are used to show a character's feelings. To make a digital character speak, the animator moves the lips of a computer model to match the pre-recorded speech. Character animators also move other parts of the computer model's face, such as ears and eyebrows, to show various emotions, such as sadness or excitement.

Controlling movements

As we have seen, a character model usually consists of a virtual stick model, a bit like a skeleton, with an outer wire frame mesh forming the outer shape of the character. Just as our own movements are controlled by our skeletons, the movements of virtual models are also controlled by their internal skeletons. The position of the major joints in the character's skeleton, such as its elbows, wrists, neck, and knees, are defined by coordinates or control points. These control points are called **avars** (animation variables). To make a character's inner skeleton move, an animator changes the position of these avars on the computer.

Shrek is such a believable character because we can see his many changing emotions through the detailed animations of his body postures and facial expressions.

Controlling facial expressions

Avars are also used to control the movement of the wire frame mesh that forms the outer surface of the character. Animators use these avars to move a character's lips and eyebrows, and to create the facial expressions and other subtle movements of a character model. Depending on the range of movements, emotions, and expressions needed, some character models have many hundreds of these control points. The character Woody from *Toy Story* had over 100 avars just to control his facial expressions.

Computer puppetry

By using control points to control the movements of 3D models, computer animators do the same kind of work as traditional puppeteers with string puppets. These traditional artists create movement in their puppets using strings, which are attached to various parts of the puppet. The points where the strings attach to the puppet are much like the system of control points within digital models.

Wearing motion capture equipment, Andy Serkis acted out all of Gollum's movements in every scene of *The Lord of the Rings* trilogy. The movement of the small lights attached to his blue suit was precisely tracked by special cameras.

Motion capture

One of the most fascinating techniques used by computer animators is called **motion capture**. Motion capture equipment is used to digitally record the natural movements of people and animals, which are then used to animate computer-generated models.

Here's how it works. An actor wears a dark, tight-fitting suit similar to a diving suit. On the surface of the suit there are special markers at numerous points, most importantly at major joints such as the shoulders, elbows, wrists, and knees. These markers can be reflective stickers, small lights, or even white ping pong balls. The markers are clearly visible and stand out against the actor's body.

The actor's movements are filmed by a camera, or sometimes by many cameras from different angles. The motion capture software recognizes only the markers being filmed. The movements of the markers can then be "attached" to a virtual 3D model so that it moves naturally, in exactly the same way as the real actor.

Performance capturing

Motion capture equipment can also be used to record facial expressions, which allows the performances of real actors to be captured and used to animate digital characters. For example, in the 2005 animated film *The Polar Express*, real actors performed their roles while wearing motion capture gear. Their facial expressions and performances were recorded and used to animate the virtual characters on-screen.

After bringing Gollum to life, Andy Serkis studied the behaviour of gorillas before performing the many facial expressions for the giant gorilla in the 2005 film *King Kong*.

Try it yourself

You will need a friend to help you. Stick glow-in-the-dark stickers at various points on your friend's clothes. The idea is to track the movement of all body parts, so make sure you mark the arms, legs, and all major joints (elbows, shoulders, and knees), as well as the hands and feet. Then, dim the lights and ask your friend to move around. Ask them to try different types of motion such as clapping their hands, boxing, or jumping up and down. When watching the movement, you'll see how the glow-in-the-dark stickers seem to show the movement of your friend's whole body. If you have access to a video camera, you can even film it like the professionals do.

Special effects animation

Animating character models is just one form of animation in the CGI process. Special effects animation is the art of animating elements in a film or game that are not characters, such as vehicles, drifting clouds, flames, falling rain, and rushing water. Special effects animation is an important part of creating a realistic computer-generated experience. Making these elements appear to move realistically is the work of special effects animators.

Traditional special effects

Visual effects have been used in films since the earliest days of film-making. In the past, special effects such as flames or smoke were often drawn, painted, or added photographically directly on to film after filming.

It looks as if James Bond narrowly escaped a fiery doom in this scene from *007: The World is Not Enough,* but this explosion was created as digital special effects and added to the live film.

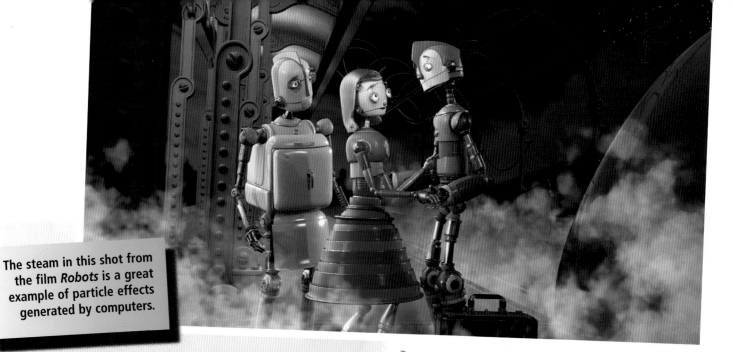

Computer-generated illusions

Today, special effects are mostly added on-screen after filming using computer-generated images. Using computer software and virtual 3D models, special effects animators create all kinds of effects from virtual lighting and swirling mist to fires and violent explosions.

Special effects animation is often used to show spectacular effects that would be too difficult or too expensive to create in the real world. For example, if a film script calls for a massive earthquake in the middle of a large city, it would be too destructive and expensive to knock down real buildings. Instead, exact virtual replicas of buildings can be created on computers and made to look as if they are crumbling to the ground.

Particle effects

Special effects animators often need to create the illusion of natural phenomena such as rainfall, snow, and fog. These types of graphics are called "particle effects". Particle effects are also used to create the illusion of fire, smoke, and other gaseous substances.

Case history: from 1977 to 2005

The technology of special effects has changed dramatically over the years. A good way to understand how the technology works is by looking at how the first and last *Star Wars* films were made. The first film, *Star Wars* (later retitled *Star Wars Episode IV: A New Hope*), was created by filming and animating miniature plastic models of x-wing fighters and imperial star destroyers. The lighting was real and produced by electric lights in a film studio. Special effects such as light sabres and lasers were created by drawing them directly on to the film. By the time the last film was made almost 30 years later, the models of fighters and other ships were digital rather than plastic miniatures. The lighting was almost entirely virtual, and the special effects were created on computers rather than on film.

Colour and texture

While computer animators perfect the movements of characters and other elements in games and films, it is up to other artists to make the artwork actually look like the real thing. One of the final art stages in the CGI process is when graphic artists apply colours, textures, and surface detail to the numerous models and illustrations within a film or computer game.

Applying colour to a computer model or illustration is a bit like painting a real surface, only it is done on the computer. Artists often use colours that are built into their software programs, which allows them to mix and match colours until they find just the right one. A surface that has just colour, however, may look unnatural because it lacks a realistic texture.

To compare colour and texture, think of an orange. An orange-coloured sphere doesn't look like the fruit unless it has the many bumps and dimples of orange peel. All surfaces have textures, from the smooth shininess of metal to the rough dullness of tree bark. Recreating these textures is essential to making digital artwork seem realistic.

Cloning colours and textures

CGI artists often use colours and textures from photographs. This is done by a process called **cloning**. A piece of a digital photograph is copied and then cloned on to the surface of a computer model or illustration.

Rendering

The final step in the CGI process is called **rendering**. This is when all the various components of a computer-generated scene – the models and illustrations, animations and special effects, the layers of colours and textures – are brought together into the final images we see on-screen. The process involves computer software that takes into account all the elements within a single frame and presents them in a way that looks real.

Real-time rendering

The main difference between film animation and computer game animation is in the rendering process. CGI made for films goes through a long rendering process before we see it on-screen. In computer games, however, the images we see must be processed immediately as we're playing the game. This is called **real-time rendering**.

Render farms

Rendering the thousands of frames that make up a film takes a lot of computer power. Rooms full of computers are needed to render an entire film. These are called render farms The rendering for the film *Madagascar*, for example, required a render farm running constantly for a year and a half!

One of the reasons the film *Madagascar* took so long to render is Alex the lion's detailed mane, made up of many thousands of individual hairs.

The process of creating computer-generated images for films and computer games involves many stages, but what tools are needed by the artists and what software is needed to bring their artwork to life?

Traditional art tools

The artwork created in the early stages of CGI development comes in many different **media**. Concept art and storyboards can be created just with a pencil and paper. But because concept art and storyboards serve as guides for later stages, they are often created in greater detail.

Charcoals can be used to show the detail of lighter and darker shades within a drawing. Concept artists may also create paintings and illustrations using vibrant colours, which will guide the digital artists as they add colours to computer models and illustrations.

Concept artists often use paints such as acrylics and gouache. Gouache is a special type of watercolour paint that reproduces well when copied digitally. Rather than using paper, some artists paint on thick canvases that provide a better base for their artwork.

Sculptures depicting characters or environmental structures need to be very detailed because digital artists usually copy them in their exact forms. These sculptures are often created using clay. Sometimes they are cast in urethane resin, a kind of liquid plastic that hardens into a solid shape.

Computer accessories

Scanners are essential tools for artists in the creation of computer-generated images. A simple flatbed scanner can transfer a drawing or painting on to a computer so that it can be worked with digitally.

Another key tool for artists is a **graphics tablet**. This tool is used in place of a computer mouse. You use a stylus pen (which looks much like an ordinary pen or pencil) to draw on the electronic board or tablet. The stylus pen controls the curser on your screen and allows you to draw and paint on-screen in a much more natural way than you can with a mouse.

2D software

As we have seen, some of the elements in a computer game or film scene are created with 2D graphics software. For example, 2D software is used to create 2D digital illustrations and for applying colours and textures to the surfaces of 3D computer models.

Photoshop and *Corel Graphics Suite* are two of the most commonly used 2D graphics software packages, but there are many others, including *Flash*, which is often used for 2D animations on the web.

A concept artist's tools can be as simple as a pencil and paper and a well-lit surface on which to draw sketches.

3D software

As with 2D software, there are many 3D computer graphics software packages. Two of the most popular are *Maya* and *3D Studio Max*.

Modelling programs usually provide basic 3D objects as starting points for building models. These objects include 3D shapes such as spheres, cylinders, and cones. For example, a modeller who is building a character from scratch may use a sphere for the character's head and cylinders for the character's body and limbs.

Wire frame models created using 3D software can be rotated within the computer so that they can be viewed and worked on from all sides. The various points within a wire frame model can be moved simply by clicking on a point and dragging with the mouse. This is how modellers "sculpt" the shapes of their models.

All-in-one packages

Many versions of the latest 3D software are all-in-one packages that allow not only the building of 3D models, but also animation, lighting, shading, colouring, and texturing.

Tutorials

Some software companies offer free tutorials and software downloads, making it fairly easy for anyone to learn the basics of 3D modelling, texturing, and animation, as well as other types of computer art skills. There are also websites that offer free tutorials, but the best place to go is usually a software company's official website.

3D software is used to build and animate characters and other models. Each model is an individual computer file created separately from the rest. This artist is working on a *Harry Potter* computer game.

In this scene from *The Lord of the Rings: Return of the King*, the elephants were created digitally using *Massive* software.

Cutting edge

The world of computer graphics can be a confusing place for an artist, especially with new tools and software coming out every year. Luckily, the most cutting-edge tools and software are becoming easier to use. So you don't have to be a computer whizz to be an artist in the field of computer graphics. A great animator, for example, is not necessarily a person who is skilled with computers. With easy-to-use software, the animator can focus on the art of animation rather than trying to master a computer program.

Massive

Peter Jackson's studio WETA created the 3D software called *Massive*. The software was used to create digital armies of mythical monsters to march through Middle Earth in *The Lord of the Rings* trilogy. This software was also used to create crowds of New Yorkers in WETA's *King Kong* film, made in 2005. The software recreates thousands of images by cloning them and randomly changing the appearance and movements of the characters, so that seen as a group, they appear to be individuals each looking and behaving differently.

Inside the industry

Cutting-edge tools and software help to bring computer-generated images to life, but none of this is possible without the talented artists who create the artwork. Now let's look inside the professional world of computer graphics and find out about some of the artists who create what we see.

The development team

The creation of a computer game or a film that relies on computer-generated imagery may take several years. For each CGI project, a **development team** is formed. This may include numerous artists who will work on different parts of the project. Artists are typically given responsibility for certain characters, scenes, or game elements rather than working on every part of a game or film. This is because numerous individual pieces of art go into a game or film from the concept stage to the final images. Creating each piece of art can take many hours or days, and sometimes even weeks and months.

Development teams include concept illustrators, storyboard artists, sculptors, modellers, and animators. They also include other professionals with art-related roles. A designer's role is to maintain an overall vision of how the various art components within a film scene or game come together. A lead artist or art director is usually in charge of the whole team of artists, which varies in size depending on the size of the project. The overall leader of a game development project is the producer or project manager, who oversees an extended team of computer programmers and others.

Working as part of a team

Professional artists must create art that works for the whole development team and sometimes the art has to be approved by other people outside the development team, such as the publishers of a game. Artists sometimes need to compromise and create art that is different from the art they would create if they were making all the decisions.

The pipeline

The various stages of artwork and computer graphics that go into making the final product is called the "pipeline". It is important for artists to know how they fit into the pipeline so that their artwork can be passed on to others further down the line.

Andy Kerridge, on the left, and Simon Phipps on the right, were the designers of the computer game *Harry Potter and the Prisoner of Azkaban*. Here they are seen in the office of Electronic Arts UK, the developers of the game.

Film graphics pioneers

Two studios leading the way in the development of CGI for films are Industrial Light & Magic and Pixar Animation Studios.

Industrial Light & Magic (ILM)

ILM is the most famous special effects studio in the world. Located in San Francisco, California, the studio was founded in 1975 during the creation of the original *Star Wars* film, which was released in 1977. As well as the *Star Wars* trilogy, the studio has created special effects for over 200 other films. Many of these films have represented important advancements in CGI, from the water creature in *The Abyss* to the latest cutting-edge effects.

Profile: Roger Guyett

Originally from the United Kingdom, Roger Guyett began his career working on TV commercials in London. He joined ILM in 1994 and worked on a number of innovative films, including two *Harry Potter* movies. As Visual Effects Supervisor, he led a team of digital artists at ILM for *Star Wars III: Revenge of the Sith*. With all the hi-tech tools at ILM, Roger still recognizes that it is the artists that do the real work. "It's not the technology that really creates the effect – it's the people with the right imagination."

The animation team at Pixar: it takes a large group of talented animators to create the computer-generated images for films like *Monsters Inc.* and *The Incredibles*.

The terrifying deep-sea anglerfish in *Finding Nemo* began with sketches and sculptures by Greg Dykstra and other artists at Pixar.

Pixar

Pixar Animation Studios actually started out as the animation department at ILM. Since forming its own studio in 1986, Pixar has helped create a new generation of 3D computer-animated films, including *Toy Story*, *Finding Nemo*, and *The Incredibles*.

Traditional art plays a very important part in the development process at Pixar. The studio walls are covered with sketches and vividly coloured concept artworks. These establish the look and feel of a film long before digital artists begin their work on computers. For *Monsters Inc.*, sculptors created at least a dozen detailed versions of Sullivan, the lead monster, before they found the right one.

Profile: Greg Dykstra

Greg Dykstra is a sculptor and character designer who started with Pixar during the development of *Finding Nemo*. He sculpted many characters, including the fearsome deep-sea anglerfish that the heroes meet deep in the ocean. Greg describes how he works: "I build the armature, a kind of wire skeleton. After I make the armature, I apply oil-based clay and build up the big shapes. Then I play with the forms, trying to refine the contours, and explore design possibilities until it feels right."

Game developers

Two of the most successful game development studios are Electronic Arts and Ubisoft.

Ubisoft

Founded in France in 1986, Ubisoft has grown into a worldwide company with many studios around the world, from Austin, Texas, to Shanghai, China. Over 3,000 people work for Ubisoft and it is one of the largest publishers of video and computer games in the world. Ubisoft has created games such as *Myst* and *Brothers in Arms*.

Storylines are very important at Ubisoft. The company has a staff of professional writers to provide stories and characters that draw users into the game world. They have even worked with famous authors such as Tom Clancy, who creates storylines for combat games, such as *Splinter Cell* and *Ghost Recon*.

Ubisoft games are developed by creative teams that include storytellers, concept artists, designers, animators, and programmers working to ensure that the various elements of each game come together smoothly.

Profile: Patrick Fortier

Patrick Fortier is Creative Director at Ubisoft in Montreal, Canada. He joined Ubisoft in 1997, and has worked on a 3D version of the classic game *Myst*. He admits that creating games is not always easy work, but enjoys hearing from players. "It [takes] a lot of effort to get there, but when we speak to enthusiastic fans on forums, it makes all our efforts that much more worth it!"

Electronic Arts UK

Electronic Arts UK (EAUK), based in Chertsey, near London, has developed many successful games, including the latest *Harry Potter* games.

The art department at EAUK includes concept artists and texture artists, as well as modellers and animators. Concept artists create the visual ideas for environments, characters, and other elements. They also create the storyboards. Texture artists create the surfaces we see within the game – what EAUK calls the "skin of the game".

The headquarters of EAUK looks rather like the kind of building that might feature in one of their games. The campus includes sports fields and an arcade room to keep the artists inspired.

Profile: Lee Robinson

Lee Robinson is the Lead Concept Artist at EAUK. He has a degree in vehicle design, but he now creates computer games rather than cars. He and his team of concept artists create the characters, environments, buildings, and vehicles in EAUK's games. "Our role is to provide the first visual view into the game design, where we provide visually stimulating ideas for the creation of the game world … This is an exciting part of the process and requires a passion for ideas and teamwork."

Beyond games and films

The computer graphics industry is a rapidly growing business. CGI is not just used for computer games and films. Many, if not most, of the commercials you see on television use some kind of computer-generated art. But it is not only advertisers that are making the industry grow.

Adventure rides and attractions in theme parks have been developed with built-in CGI. **Virtual-reality simulators** enable visitors to interact with 3D virtual environments. These environments are created with the same kinds of models and artwork used to create computer games and film graphics.

Freelancers

Some computer graphics artists are freelancers. Rather than staying with one studio, freelancers sign up with a studio for a single project and then move on to another project, which may be at a different studio. Some people enjoy the freedom of short-term jobs, and find that being freelance allows them to do something different with each assignment.

Film studios often use freelancers because they do not need the skills of these artists on a permanent basis. They may need artists with different creative talents for each project. Many freelance CGI artists start out working on short-term projects in advertising and then move on to films.

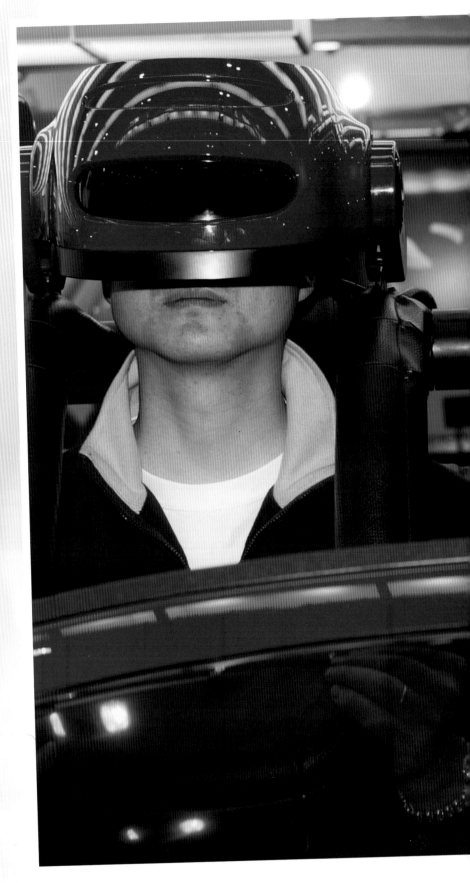

Your portfolio

It is not easy to get work on a feature film or in game development, but a good **portfolio** will help. Your portfolio is a collection of your artwork that you want others to see. If you do not already have a portfolio, you could start one with the artwork you have created in the "Try it yourself" activities in this book.

In the professional world, a portfolio is a showcase of an artist's skills. The artwork is kept in a folder or a case for display and shown to people who might employ the artist, either in a permanent job or for a particular project. Animators and 3D model-builders also need video recordings of their work. These recordings are called **showreels**. They act a bit like a digitized portfolio.

Professional advice

John Miles of Electronic Arts UK has the following advice: "Create a good, concise portfolio or showreel. Don't put everything in it. Put only your best work in it, and don't just present one type of medium ... you should make an effort to include traditional art media, such as drawing, sculpture, or painting."

Virtual-reality headgear turns an amusement park ride into a 3D adventure in which a viewer's entire range of vision is surrounded by computer graphics.

Do you think you would enjoy a career as an artist working on CGI for films or computer games? There are many ways you can prepare yourself and take your interests further.

An artist's education

If you want to work with computer-generated art, you need to begin by studying traditional art. Even the simplest art projects are great ways to learn the basic techniques that computer graphics artists need to understand, such as how to use perspective, colour, lighting, and shading.

It is important to learn how to draw recognizable characters such as people, animals, and other creatures, as well as objects such as buildings, cars, and other machines. It also helps to practise drawing environments of all kinds. Any kind of sculpting or modelling is great preparation for 3D computer modelling.

Before you can get a job as a computer graphics artist, it is important to learn how to create traditional art.

Developing your talents

As you move on in your education, you will find more and more opportunities to develop your artistic talents. You may have the opportunity to study more in-depth art courses on character drawing, sculpting, animation, and 3D design. Your school might have an art club – think about joining so you can share ideas with other artists.

Use your school's computers as much as you can and ask your teacher or librarian about the software available to you. Many schools have software such as *Photoshop* and schools often have computer or graphics clubs.

Get to know the world of art

The more you learn about art, the better prepared you will be to create great art yourself. Look at classic works of art and explore how artists created their masterpieces. For example, think about how they dealt with lighting in a portrait or created the illusion of depth in a landscape. You should also study the works of current graphic artists and other artists.

One of the best places to find art is in museums and art galleries. Find out about museums and galleries in your area – you may even find ones with exhibits of CGI. You should also study the different kinds of CGI you see all the time, while playing games and watching television.

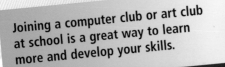
Joining a computer club or art club at school is a great way to learn more and develop your skills.

Learn about the world around you

An education in art is important for all future artists, but other subject areas can be just as helpful. Studying science will help you become a better artist. For example, learning about geology in earth science may help if you are creating 3D models of landscapes. Biology helps you understand how people and creatures look and move, so your drawings and animations can be more realistic.

Finding inspiration

In history and English classes, you may find out about events and stories that might inspire the plots for films or video games. You cannot create art for the latest World War II combat game unless you know what soldiers and their weapons looked like in the 1940s. You may also find inspiration from studying mythology and learning about legendary heroes and the monsters they battled.

In order to create virtual models of dinosaurs and other creatures, it's important to learn all you can about skeletons and how creatures move. Natural history museums are great places to expand your knowledge.

An art degree

Obtaining an art degree from a college or university can be your ticket to a career as a computer graphics artist. A college or university art curriculum involves in-depth studies of art techniques and theories.

Degree courses often involve studying art history and classic architecture to see how artists have created great works of art in the past. Students on degree courses also spend a lot of time and effort on single projects, much like a professional artist does. If you do not have a portfolio by the time you enter college, you will definitely have one by the time you gain your degree.

Look carefully at all forms of computer-generated art you see. Play lots of computer games and watch lots of films!

Game development courses

A growing number of universities are now offering academic courses that focus on game development. These courses cover all areas of development, from game design, programming, and storytelling, to traditional areas of art such as colour theory and sculpting. On many of these courses it is possible to focus on a single speciality such as animation.

Internships

Internships are programmes for secondary-school, college, and university students to work in a professional studio. These jobs sometimes pay a small hourly wage, but often there is no pay. However, the true value is in the real-world experience that these internships provide. Most internships go to college students, but there are some for lucky secondary-school students as well.

Glossary

2D having two dimensions – width and height. When something is 2D, it has no depth and looks flat.

3D having three dimensions – width, height, and depth. 3D is short for "three dimensional". When something is drawn or painted to look 3D, it looks solid, not flat.

animation technique that creates the illusion of movement by displaying a series of still images

armature solid internal frame that supports a sculpture or statue

avar control point within a digital wire frame model

CGI (computer-generated imagery) general term for computer modelling and animation, especially in the creation of 3D digital artwork

cloning in computer graphics, a technique in which an artist copies images, colours, or textures and applies them to a digital model or illustration

comic strip series of illustrations that tell a story

computer graphics general term for art and other images generated by computers

concept art sketches, drawings, and paintings that are created to express the visual concepts and ideas of a story

development team group of artists and other professionals who work together on a given project, usually at a film or game development studio

digital relating to the way information is stored on a computer. A digital artist produces artwork using a computer and a digital image is an image generated by a computer.

digital model virtual 3D object created on a computer

feature-length film full-length film, lasting an hour or more, as opposed to a short film, which usually lasts less than 10–15 minutes

graphics tablet common computer accessory that allows users to control the on-screen curser with a pencil-like drawing tool

illusion something that looks real, but is not

live-action film film that is filmed as photography with real actors and within the real world, as opposed to animated films, which are made from illustrations and models

maquette detailed sculpture showing a character in a specific pose

media in the world of art, the different types of material used to create art

motion capture process of recording motion with digital photography and using the recorded motion to animate digital models

perspective the way in which objects appear in relation to each other. Using the rules of perspective can make 2D illustrations appear 3D.

photorealistic term given to artwork that looks like a photograph or a photographic film

portfolio collection of an artist's creative work to show to possible employers and others

real-time rendering process in which video images are rendered immediately as they happen

render farm computer cluster used to render computer-generated imagery (CGI), typically for films and television special effects

rendering processing of a picture in which computer data is transformed into visual images

scan copy an image to a computer file (to scan); or the file itself (a scan)

scanner machine used to scan files on to a computer

showreel computer file or video footage showing the models and animations of digital artists

special effects visual effects added to a film or television show. Special effects is a general term for CGI in live-action films and special effects animation is the process of animating anything that moves in a film that is not a character.

stop motion form of animation that uses physical models, made out of clay or other materials. The models are photographed frame-by-frame and their position is altered slightly in-between each frame. When the frames are shown in quick succession, the models appear to be in motion.

storyboard series of illustrations laid out a bit like a comic strip, showing the plot, action, characters, and setting of a film. Storyboards provide a visual idea of how scenes will come together as the story is being acted out.

texture the look and feel of a surface; in art and computer graphics, the way in which surfaces are made to look through the use of colours, shading, and lighting

virtual something that does not physically exist, but uses software to make it appear "real"

virtual-reality simulator equipment such as a headset with a screen inside that generates computer-generated images of objects or 3D environments that can be interacted with and seem real

wire frame surface model represented by points and lines, usually segmented into mathematically precise shapes such as triangles

Find out more

Milestones in computer game and film graphics

1961: The first computer game, *Spacewar*, is invented

1966: The first home computer game, *Odyssey*, is released

1971: *Computer Space*, the first major arcade game, is released

1972: *Pong*, the first mass-market home computer game to reach a large audience, is released

1976: The film *Futureworld* features the first use of 3D CGI in a major film

1977: The *Atari 2600* game system, the first home game console to play multiple game cartridges, is introduced

1982: The film *Tron*, about characters inside a computer game, features the first wide use of computer graphics in a film; the game developer Electronic Arts is founded

1985: The first character created using CGI features in the film, *Young Sherlock Holmes*

1989: A photorealistic water creature, created entirely using 3D CGI, features in the film, *The Abyss*

1990: The film *Total Recall* is the first to use motion capture techniques for CGI characters

1993: *Jurassic Park* is the first film to feature dozens of CGI characters (the dinosaurs)

1995: Pixar Animation Studios releases *Toy Story*, the first feature-length computer-animated film

1999: *Star Wars Episode I* features over 50 CGI characters, more than had ever been created for a single live-action film

2002: *The Sims*, a game featuring 3D characters, becomes the best-selling computer game ever

2004: The animated film *The Polar Express* becomes the first film to use performance capture techniques for every character

2005: The *Xbox 360*, a game system able to produce photorealistic graphics for computer games, is released

More books to read

Don Bluth's Art of Storyboard, by Don Bluth (DH Press, 2004)

Game Design for Teens, by Eric Nunamaker, Scott Pugh, and Les Pardew (Premier Press, 2004)

Basic Drawing for Games, by Les Pardew (Course Technology, 2005)

Game Art for Teens, by Les Pardew (Thomson/Course Technology, 2005)

The Art of Star Wars Episode III: Revenge of the Sith, by J.W. Rinzler (Ebury Press, 2005)

Character Animation in 3D: Use Traditional Drawing Techniques to Produce Stunning CGI Animation, by Steve Roberts (Focal Press, 2004)

Attack of the Killer Video Book: Tips and Tricks for Young Directors, by Mark Shulman, Hazlitt Krog, Martha Newbigging (illustrator) (Annick Press, 2004)

Useful websites

http://www.igda.org/breakingin/profiles.htm
An International Game Developers Association website providing career profiles of people who work in the computer game industry.

http://computer.howstuffworks.com/
Insert "3D graphics" in the search box and follow the link to "How 3-D Graphics work", for a website providing clear information on 3D graphics.

http://moca.virtual.museum
A museum of computer art on the web, with many examples of 3D and computer-generated art.

http://www.electronicarts.co.uk
The website of the game developers Electronic Arts UK (see page 45).

http://www.ilm.com
The website of Industrial Light & Magic (see page 42).

http://www.pixar.com
The website of Pixar Animation Studios (see page 43).

http://ubi.com
The website of the game developers Ubisoft (see page 44).

Software

Adobe Photoshop and *Corel Graphics Suite* are two of the most popular 2D software packages used to create 2D illustrations as backdrops and to add colour and texture to the surfaces of 3D models.

Maya and *3D Studio Max* are the two most popular 3D software packages used to built and animate 3D digital models.

Disclaimer
All the Internet addresses (URLs) given in this book were valid at the time of going to press. However, owing to the dynamic nature of the Internet, some addresses may have changed or sites may have ceased to exist since publication. While the author, packager, and publishers regret any inconvenience this may cause readers, no responsibility for any such change can be accepted by the author, packager, or publishers.

Index

Titles in the *Art off the wall* series include:

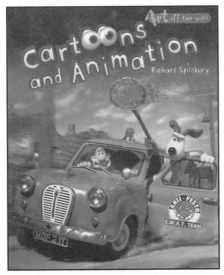

Hardback   978-0-431-01473-9

Hardback   978-0-431-01472-2

Hardback   978-0-431-01474-6

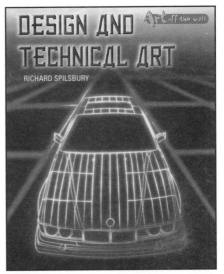

Hardback   978-0-431-01475-3

Hardback   978-0-431-01476-0

Find out about other titles from Heinemann Library on our website www.heinemann.co.uk/library